KU-349-482

PENTICTON,

BRITISH COLUMBIA:

Silhouette Of Four Seasons

To every thing there is a season...
(Ecclesiastes 3)

Written and Compiled by Penticton Writers and Publishers

Janelle Breese–Biagioni Lorraine Pattison
Yasmin John–Thorpe Penny Smith

Dedicated to the City of Penticton

Penticton, British Columbia: Silhouette Of Four Seasons

Published by The City of Penticton, June 1998

Written and compiled by Penticton Writers and Publishers

Cover photo by Rod Penfold
Cover photo inserts by Stuart Bish, Gerhard Kahrmann, Laure Neish, & Chris Cornett
Cover design/digital imaging/layout by Stuart Bish M.P.A., Photography/Design

Photo Editor Ellen Boerboom

Text Editor Hugh Lines

Page Layout/Typography by James Shand

ISBN 0–9698449–5–6

1. Penticton (B.C.)—Pictorial works. 2. Penticton (B.C.) I. Breese–Biagioni, Janelle, 1956–
II. Penticton Writers and Publishers. III. Penticton (B.C.)
FC3849.P4P43 1998 971.1'5'00222 C98–910407–9 F1089.5.P45P46 1998

Printed and bound in Canada by Friesens

The City of Penticton
171 Main Street,
Penticton, B.C.,
V2A 5A9 Canada

With Our Thanks

Unable to refuse a challenge, the four co–founding members of Penticton Writers and Publishers readily accepted the task of compiling, writing, and producing a prestigious pictorial book for the City of Penticton. This we found out was to be no small task. Our request for photo submissions produced literally hundreds from which to choose. In narrowing this collection to 70 plus photos, each worth a "thousand words," we saw the city through new eyes. Our appreciation for the enormous responsibility of presenting the best of what Penticton has to offer brought us great satisfaction.

Special thanks to: The City of Penticton and staff, especially her Worship Mayor Beth Campbell, Tim Wood, and Richard Ramsay; the City resource committee; Rory McIvor of the Penticton Library; the Penticton & Wine Country Chamber of Commerce; Tourism Penticton; Sumac Ridge Estate Winery Ltd. and Cherry Lane Shopping Centre. Special thanks also extended to the media: the Penticton Herald and Penticton Western News Advertiser; CHBC Television; CKOR Radio; CIGV Radio; Alan Thom, host of "Around Penticton," and Shaw Cable Television. Randy Manuel and staff of the R.N. Atkinson Museum have contributed greatly with advice and use of the archives room and collections. Their support, knowledge, and assistance was more than we ever expected. Many, many thanks.

We would like to express our sincerest gratitude to Stuart Bish for his professional expertise and his willingness to go above and beyond what was required, ensuring this book would be the best.

We are grateful to all contributing photographers, in particular David Szabo who went out of his way to take last minute photos, safeguarding our commitment to portray the "four seasons." Also, our thanks to the photo editor Ellen Boerboom, text editor Hugh Lines, and Photographer Hugo Redivo for their valued input. Thanks to Laser Images for their care in scanning slides.

Many thanks to the businesses and individuals who invested in this project. Without their support this book would have never been possible. We hope you enjoy this visual expression of our beautiful community.

Special thanks to Anne De Grace and Steve Thornton, authors of <u>*Nelson British Columbia In photographs*</u> for their inspiration and to the City of Vernon for their permission to include the name "Ogopogo" in the book.

Most of all, we wish to thank our families for their patience, support, and understanding.

Penticton Writers and Publishers

LETTER FROM THE MAYOR

Message from the Mayor:

Penticton, British Columbia: Silhouette Of Four Seasons, truly captures the spirit, beauty and diversity of Penticton in its magnificent Okanagan Valley setting. Nestled in the Okanagan Highlands and the Thompson Plateau between two lakes at the northern tip of the Columbian River Basin, Penticton has unique geography, climate, people and history as depicted photographically in this book. From vineyards to wineries, from water skis to snow skis, from Wine and Peach Festivals to Jazz Festivals and from the Subaru Ironman Canada Triathalon Championship to a walk on the beach, Penticton offers a rich quality of life for everyone.

As a "Place to Live Forever" Penticton embraces the four seasons in work and play. The fragrance of spring wild flowers, the caress of summer sun, the bounty of fall harvest and the silent snowfall of mountain winter, all shape Penticton. This wonderful book is proof that a picture is worth a thousand words. Feel the excitement, character and extraordinary beauty of Penticton through its pages, as the seasons change.

Beth Campbell
Mayor of Penticton

Stuart Bish M.P.A.

The word is out!

Chatelaine magazine recently declared Penticton the best place to live in Canada – a "secret" we already knew! We boast a safe and pristine environment, preserving much of the natural heritage of our city which is becoming internationally renown as a resort destination. Tourism has been highly promoted since the early 1900s and has proved to be the major base in our economic development.

Over the years Penticton has grown to include other types of industries. Furniture, home manufacturing and lumber re–manufacturing have become an important part of our economy, providing year–round employment for hundreds of people.

Doug Cox

Penticton, the largest community in the South Okanagan Valley, is located 5 hours driving time east of Vancouver (a mere 45 minute flight from Vancouver to Penticton International Airport), 8 hours west of Calgary, Alberta, and 35 minutes north of the Canada–U.S. border. The lifestyle of our 30,000 plus residents is the envy of many. Our unique community spirit has locals turning out in large numbers to volunteer for special events. These have included the B.C. Summer Games, the Soroptomist Home Show, the B.C. Festival of the Arts, and the Penticton Kiwanis Music Festival. Numerous service clubs provide much needed funds and support for community based projects, including hospital equipment for our modern medical complex, children's playgrounds, sports facilities and assistance to non–profit organizations.

This spirit holds true even in difficult times. On several occasions, the residents have pooled their resources to help those in need. One such example occurred in July 1994, when the disastrous Garnet Fire wiped out 18 homes and 5500 hectares of forest. While thousands courageously battled nature's fury, others opened their doors to traumatized humans and animals.

Sports tournaments, spring and fall festivals, symposiums, and theatre arts keep both residents and visitors hopping.

One can enjoy night clubs and ethnic cuisine, visit art galleries and the Museum Library Complex, or take in lectures and gala charity events. Romantics can steal away aboard a houseboat for a moonlit cruise or stroll along the promenade to the Penticton Rose Garden. There, they may visit the garden's famous Sun Dial or the bed of red roses honouring Penticton's Japanese sister city, Ikeda. A watchful eye may glimpse resident beavers, Bud and Rosie.

The Penticton Trade & Convention Centre was the first free standing facility of its type built in Canada and remains the largest of its kind in the Okanagan Valley. With over 30 years of service, the centre easily accommodates up to

Jeanette Beaven

3,500 delegates and is booked year round. At the close of the conference day, participants can kick back and relax with the comforts of home found on Okanagan Beach's Sunset Strip or visit nearby health clubs, tennis courts, major shopping malls, coffee houses and a variety of golf courses.

A leisurely stroll down colourful Front Street (photo) featuring heritage buildings and specialty shops is a must! Maybe your preference is viewing exotic flowers or tasting chocolate–covered cherries and blueberries. Then, this Penticton central location makes for pleasant outings.

The Ornamental Gardens in Summerland, The White Lake Observatory near Kaleden and Tickleberry's (specialty confections and the "best ice cream") in Okanagan Falls, are only a short trip away.

Longer excursions to The Grist Mill in Keremeos and the O'Keefe Historical Ranch in Vernon may include many interesting stops at natural animal habitats, fruit stands or estate wineries.

Recognized for its picturesque setting of rugged mountains and warm water lakes, Penticton's long hot summers and mild winters are a delight for guests and residents.

This serene setting in the heart of the wine and fruit belt makes our city a premier vacation paradise and a *Place to Live Forever.*

THE PLACE TO STAY FOREVER

"Like a Phoenix rising out of the ashes" an oasis emerged from under a receding ice–cap. Gentle sloping benches of sagebrush, bordered by clay cliffs, gave way to a lush valley bottom of vegetation and grasses. A glacial lake, having been split in two, was linked by an ever–flowing, serpentine river, giving birth to an array of wild flowers, grassy reeds, fish, and wild game. A land was born!

The Okanagan Indians, a branch of the Salish Indians, were the first to come upon this land. They named it *Pen–Tak–Tin*, 'A Place to Live Forever'.

They camped on the shores of Dog (Skaha) and Okanagan Lakes hunting the plentiful deer, elk, bighorn sheep, fishing for salmon and trout, and trapping. Today, the Natives' descendants are the Penticton Indian Band.

In 1866, Thomas Ellis, a young, visionary Irish immigrant was the first white settler. He staked his claim, built a cattle empire and planted the first fruit trees. He and his wife, Wilhemina (Wade), raised nine children, forming the core of the new community.

Penticton Museum Archives

By 1892 Tom Ellis had built the "Penticton Hotel" on a hill overlooking the government wharf. It quickly became the busiest social centre of town. Within walking distance was the first street, Smith (Front Street – photo). It was quite modern for the times: graded, lined with wooden sidewalks and lit by coal oil lamps.

The first stern–wheeler, the "S.S. Aberdeen," appeared on Okanagan Lake in the early1890s. Movement of goods and services improved greatly, bringing settlers, miners, and traders to the area. In 1907, a group of residents formed a Board of Trade, showing foresight in promoting the area. This Board was the catalyst in advancing the arts, commerce, education, and recreation.

During that time, the larger "S.S. Okanagan" was launched, while smaller boats serviced Dog (Skaha) Lake. With the increased commercial activity and building starts, Penticton was officially established as a district municipality on December 31, 1908.

Not long after becoming a municipality, Penticton's first fruit trees, the majority of which were apple, began to produce, creating a long standing industry. Once picked, this delicious fruit was wrapped and crated in boxes made from local Ponderosa pine for shipment to many Canadian and international locations.

The prestigious Incola Hotel was completed by the CPR in 1912 and continued operation for nearly 70 years. Saturday nights rocked at the new Aquatic Club with its three–sided deck. It was a popular place to dance the fox trot, the waltz, and the flirty Charleston. Eavesdropping children hid in the war canoes stored beneath the deck. The famous Teen Town Club, a youth organization born here, met regularly at this facility.

At the start of World War I, the luxurious "S.S. Sicamous," dubbed Queen of the Lake, arrived on the scene. One year later the Kettle Valley Railway came into service, moving freight and passengers. During World War II, an airport was built and used for wartime security. By 1947 Canadian Pacific Airlines made scheduled flights to Penticton. The 1948 opening of the Hope/Princeton Highway increased auto traffic, creating competition with passenger rail service. Rail passenger service ended in 1964 with freight service ending 25 years later.

courtesy Stewart Lyon

May 10, 1948, was a red–letter day for Penticton as it was officially declared a city. Reeve Robert Lyon became the first mayor and was presented the charter by his Excellency Viscount Alexander of Tunis, Governor General of Canada (photo). Lord Alexander was made a Freeman of the city.

Over the years Penticton pioneers knew how to have fun, whether nibbling on box lunches while cheering for their favourite horse at Queen's Park, or spending a lazy afternoon swimming, boating, fishing, hiking, or rafting down the winding Okanagan River. Another family pastime was spent watching the comical soap–box derby. Winter offered a wonderland for sleigh riding, tobogganing, and skating on the frozen lake or nearby Guernsey's Pond.

Whatever the season, Penticton has proven from one generation to the next that this is truly the *Place to Stay Forever.*

Stuart Bish M.P.A.

The birth of spring offers a spectacular display of fruit trees bursting with fragrant blossoms, of sapphire coloured lakes and of a brilliant blue sky. Naramata (a bedroom community located 14 km north of Penticton) is one of the few remaining communities to celebrate May Day with its colourful and impressive Maypole dance, an annual festival announcing spring's return.

Average Climate

2,032 hours of sunshine annually
148 frost free days
218 mm (7.85 in) rain per year
Jan. low 0 (32F) – average temperature
July high 28.6 (83F) – average temperature

Blossom & Fruit Schedule

Fruit	Blossom	Ripening
Cherries	Apr. 15 – May 10	June 25 – July 20
Peaches	Apr. 15 – May 10	July 30 – Sept. 1
Pears	Apr. 20 – May 16	Aug. 15 – Sept. 15
Prunes	Apr. 20 – May 20	Sept. 1 – Sept. 20
Apples	Apr. 25 – May 20	Aug. 1 – Oct. 10
Grapes	Apr. 25 – May 20	Sept. 5 – Oct. 10

Discover Penticton 1994

Gerhard Kahrmann

Stuart Bish M.P.A

The Penticton Golf and Country Club (opposite) is an18 hole, semi– private course with superb facilities. Its many challenges and park–like setting beckon golfers to return year after year. It is home to celebrated golfer Anna–Jane (A.J.) Eathorne and first class tournaments, such as Andy Moog & Friends Charity and Celebrity Classic. The golf season runs February through to mid–December.

courtesy Penticton Museum Les Hill collection

Each new day brings a delight. Friendships and acquaintances are renewed after sitting indoors by the fire. From birds singing to a good game of marbles, people of all ages emerge outdoors to take in the surrounding beauty. The once vacant beaches bustle with people enjoying walks or flying kites along the water's edge. Others take in horseback riding and mini–golf. A burst of activity includes junior and adult baseball, soccer, rugby, jogging, power–walking, and rollerblading. The serene, natural surrounding is also conducive to re-energizing through yoga and tai–chi. Avid campers begin scouting the perfect site in one of many provincial parks located in the Okanagan–Similkameen area.

The more adventuresome and skilled embark on a visit to Skaha Bluffs which provide a multitude of climbs catering to all levels of difficulty. Hiking and mountain biking enthusiasts enjoy many prized trails, such as the Kettle Valley Railway, Munson Mountain, and Ellis Creek Canyon.

Howie Richardson

David Szabo

On a typical afternoon police officers often can be seen taking a moment to chat with Penticton's youngest citizens. In 1998, the RCMP mark their 125th Anniversary with the new philosophy of community–based policing. It ensures a more proactive and preventative role that goes beyond typical law enforcement.

It is not uncommon to find several generations of a family enjoying an afternoon fishing or sitting on the beach having an evening picnic (photo). Those born and raised here value the quality of life offered and devote themselves to making this truly a place to stay forever. Newcomers quickly adopt this attitude of permanence.

Seniors too enjoy the healthy lifestyle, participating in a variety of indoor and outdoor settings. Many delve into new experiences which include cruising the electronic highway. Penticton has numerous gated communities catering to 'adult living' and some of the province's finest full service retirement centres.

Stuart Bish M.P.A.

Randy Manuel

This 1920s home was built by David Riordan, a daring rum–runner during the time of prohibition. It's alleged that he and the Catholic priest stored liquor in the basement of a local church before transporting the spirits by buckboard to the American border. Today, this house operates as Riordan House Bed & Breakfast.

John & Donna Ortiz (Riordan House B & B)

In the 1950s a taxi stand stood at the corner of Wade and Main. Later, a much needed department store was built by the Hudson's Bay Co., eventually becoming Zellers. After Zellers closed, the structure was gutted and refurbished as a magnificent 45,000 sq. ft. building, currently known as City Centre.

Penticton Museum Archives

Stuart Bish M.P.A.

Richard J. Cannings

Laure Neish

Year–round mild temperatures make Penticton and area the perfect site for the increasingly popular activity of bird–watching. A variety of species can be found in the natural habitat of this area. The California Quail, native to California and Oregon, was introduced to the Okanagan over 70 years ago. Today, Penticton boasts more of these little fellows per acre than anywhere else on earth. Grandparents, parents, and children can enjoy a new experience by taking in the South Okanagan Meadow Lark Bird Festival.

Gerhard Kahrmann

Laure Neish

courtesy Penticton Museum Les Hill collection

The semi–arid climate provides not only ideal soil conditions for agriculture, it also creates spectacular natural scenery. Besides the sage and sandy beaches, the South Okanagan is known for its unique flora and fauna such as the flowering cactus, fiery red sumac, delicately flowered bitterroot, wild sunflowers and poppies. Many species of wildlife, including the cougar (this one seen at a local attraction in a natural setting) are native to Penticton and its surrounding area. Of course, the most famous and sought after sighting is the distinguished lake monster, Ogopogo (facing photo).

Doug Cox

Gerhard Kahrmann

David Szabo

David Szabo

The Okanagan Summer School of the Arts (OSSA), in operation since 1960, promotes the arts to locals and visitors for a three week period each July.

Beginners and professionals who are interested in development of the arts benefit from talented instructors of music, dance, drama, screenwriting, visual arts, and much more. This is a fun–filled and inspirational experience with venues in unique classroom settings, for example dance and movement classes that take place on the beach. Creative children's programs make this a family learning experience.

The Beach Blanket Film Festival, created by local Genie nominee Nikos Theodosakis, is a trademark summer event and a distinctive celebration of Canadian films.

David Szabo

Okanagan Beach is transformed into an outdoor theatre with films projected onto a huge off–shore screen. The reflections of flickering images on the water, the sound of waves, and music from the film, are elements that combine to make this film festival unique to Canada. Bring your sandpail for the world's tastiest popcorn! It is another magical world.

Steven Tomlinson

The Square Dance Jamboree (facing page), a famous international event, is staged here on the world's largest outdoor dance floor at King's Park. Arriving a week prior to Peach Festival, 60 – 80 callers and some 2000 dancers from around the world come together to swing their partners to a whirl and a twirl… Do–Si–Do anyone?

Chris Cornett

The annual Peach Festival is one of the most popular week–long events staged in the interior. It is a celebration of our community's bounty enjoyed by the entire family.

The first Peach Festival held in August 1948 had a parade, a rodeo, a wild cow milking contest, a midway, an agricultural show and a royalty crowning. The first Queen Val–Vedette, Beverley Ann (Young) McConechy was crowned by Penticton born, Hollywood actress Alexis Smith. The title Val–Vedette is taken from three varieties of locally grown peaches: Valiant, Veteran, and Vedette.

Today, the festival continues bigger and better than ever. These five fun–packed days of family entertainment feature dances, tournaments, Kiddy's Day, fireworks, Grand Parade (see photo) and, of course, the Miss Penticton Pageant. This ambassadorship precedes the long–standing Miss Interior Pageant. The crowning of the 50th Queen Val–Vedette, Jyoti Lal was held in 1997.

Chris Cornett

A para–sail ride is a breathtaking experience. Guided by trained hands and securely equipped in a colourful parachute, the para–sailor is gently lifted from the beach of Okanagan (or Skaha) Lake by the power of a jet–engine boat, pulling her from one side of the lake to the other. After the slow descent, the para–sailor returns to where she started with hardly a drop of water on her.

Shelley R. Daly

Each year thousands of tourists flock to the sandy shores of Skaha Lake to soak up the sun and take home a great tan. Don't forget the suntan lotion! Some will join in a game of beach volleyball or tennis, while others take to the water. The ever–popular jet ski is powerful and responsive. Those who prefer a quieter activity might choose to manoeuvre a wind surfer through the lake breezes, testing their skill and agility. A great day ends with a sunset barbecue on the beach. Fun on the water is limited only by your imagination… swimming, water skiing, boating, or floating on a colourful raft … it's all here to enjoy!

courtesy Tourism Penticton Gord Wylie

Hillmen M. Holm

A summer picnic by the warm water's edge is a pleasurable way to spend a few hours. The fine sand on our beaches is clean and perfect for building magical castles and fortresses. Children always surprise us with what their pails, shovels, and imaginations can create.

The little ones enjoy fun and games at the Skaha Rotary Playworld while teens try their skills at the challenging skateboard park. The entire family can make an outing of a game of mini–golf, or take in the exciting stock car races.

After a busy day of running, playing and swimming, everyone will welcome a sip of Penticton's clean, cool, and safe water.

Nikos Theodosakis

Gerhard Kahrmann

The Okanagan River was narrow and winding until the ‘50s when (in order to control water levels) it was changed to an open 3.8 mile channel connecting the two lakes. Since then, thousands have leisurely floated down the channel in rafts and giant inner tubes. In July, a colourful Grand Raft Parade is held, ending with Mr. Muscle, Bikini, and sand castle contests on Skaha Beach.

David Szabo

David Szabo

The Subaru Ironman Canada Triathlon Championship is a premier, qualifying race for the Hawaii Ironman World Championship. It is the only Ironman Triathlon on the North American continent and is held annually in Penticton.

This endurance race is a three–discipline athletic event: a 2.4 mile (3.8 km) swim, followed by a grinding 112 mile (180.2 km) bicycle ride and finishing with an exhausting 26.2 mile (42.2 km) run. All three stages need to be completed within 17 hours to constitute an official finish.

A normal week of training for an Ironman athlete would include six miles of swimming, 200 miles on a bike, and a 35 mile run.

David Szabo

The gruelling test of strength, stamina, and time takes its toll on many. The last of the competitors exemplify determination as they continue late into the night to achieve their personal best. Many supporters remain to cheer them on.

Coming across the finish line, an inspiring Wally Hild, recent cancer survivor, successfully completed his first Ironman in just over 16 hours.

With 1,800 competitors, it takes over 4,000 local volunteers to manage this phenomenal event. Competitors register for the next year the moment the race is finished and the work begins immediately for the race committee.

Shelley R. Daly

Steven Tomlinson

Stuart Bish M.P.A.

David Szabo

A Saturday morning stroll through the farmers' market is guaranteed to bring pleasure to the keenest of shoppers. Vegetables, herbs and fruit of every colour abound, overwhelming the senses — a sure indication 'canning season' has begun.

Red Delicious apples, awaiting harvest, tempt passers–by to pluck just one from the orchard (facing page) and eagerly sink their teeth into the juicy, crisp fruit. As the saying goes, "the one which has been stolen is always sweeter."

Laure Neish

Stuart Bish M.P.A.

Penticton Herald – John Moorhouse

Put on your dancing shoes. Get out the umbrellas, top hats and walking sticks. Bid a *'Pentastic Hot Jazz Festival'* welcome to the sounds of the South as they come north.

We don't have to travel to the bayou or New Orleans to hear the sounds of Dixieland Jazz. They journey right to our doorstep, making toe–tapping, hand–clapping converts of us all. The music is alive, thriving in the hearts of local residents, even young people.

Many eagerly soak up the ambience of tinkling pianos, vibrating basses, wailing horns, plucking banjos, soulful voices... *'and all that jazz'*!

Unique indigenous services are available to students from around the globe at the En'Owkin Centre. Classes in creative writing, visual arts, and Okanagan language and history are taught.

Also at the Centre is Theytus Books, an on–site publishing house which promotes works from an indigenous perspective. And Indigenous Arts Service Organization (IASO) services and supports artists in all artistic disciplines in the province.

Members of our local Okanagan Nation (below) join in city festivals, as seen in this prize–winning creative float.

David Szabo

The Film Box

The First Nations SN'PNK'TN Pow Wow in 1997 brought Native peoples from across North America, such as the elder (above), for a gathering to celebrate dances and drums.

Welcome to Wine Country...

...where geographic location, micro–climate and rich soil offer grape growers such good conditions that Dionysus (the Greek God of wine) himself must be jealous.

David Szabo

Fall is the time for harvest and enjoyment of grape stomps and festivals, but many a discerning grower now leave the ripened fruit until the temperatures nip down to –10 C (page 44).

This process produces the unique and expensive ice wine. Each carefully picked grape is 80% water and 20% fruit, which results in an increased number being used to fill a bottle. But the taste of one of nature's best kept secrets is worth the wait and the price.

The demands for our wines helped give birth to the British Columbia Wine Country Information Centre, at 888 Westminster Ave. West (page 45), the first of its kind in Canada. The Tiffany stained glass windows were created by Maryan Dennison and Ross Hanson. The Centre offers the consumer the largest selection of the finest VQA wines in British Columbia. Over 30 area wineries listing more than 250 labels offer a diverse range from which to choose.

courtesy Sumac Ridge Estate Winery Gord Wylie

Residents and visitors flock to the City's annual Spring and Fall Wine Festivals. The Fall venue attracts thousands of wine enthusiasts, eager to participate in the consumers' tasting and voting. Gold, Silver and Bronze medals are awarded each year, catapulting the winners to new levels of recognition.

The strictest guidelines in the world, Vintner Quality Alliance(VQA), are enforced to ensure the wines from area wineries attain the highest quality. This has helped to create first class award winning wines, using such grapes as Chardonney, Gewurztraminer, Pinot Blanc (whites), and Carbenet Sauvignon, Pinot Noir, Merlot (reds), in the area's farm, estate and major wineries.

courtesy Sumac Ridge Estate Winery Gord Wylie

Stuart Bish M.P.A.

courtesy Sumac Ridge Estate Winery Gord Wylie

David Szabo

Frank Babakaiff

In a part of the city where at the turn of the century only affluent merchants and professionals once lived, this beautiful heritage residence has stood the test of time. It is a credit to its builder Mr. F.H. Latimer, one of the early municipal engineers, who constructed the house in 1906 for himself.

The current owners, Dr. and Mrs. J. J. Gibson, moved into the house in 1946. The Gibson family had lived in the area since the early 1900s, so it was no surprise when the son and his wife settled in Penticton to raise a family.

The house, sheltered through the seasons by an abundance of foliage, sits in the city's downtown core. It remains a heart–warming sight for locals and visitors. Dr. and Mrs. Gibson, both in their 80s, still reside in the heritage home.

The leaves are falling, there is a nip in the air and the pumpkin patch is full of orange Jack O' Lanterns. It must be time for those famous words..."Trick Or Treat?"

'Spooktacular' has become one of the largest and safest community–based Hallowe'en parties in Canada. The organizers, the staff of the Penticton Community Centre, took our young children off the streets and out of harm's way, placing them under one roof (The Trade and Convention Centre), where they enjoy the magic of ghosts and goblins.

Each year some 1,500 costumed kids, supervised by more than 300 enthusiastic volunteers, gobble up over 100,000 donated candies. It is a magical time not only for the 'trick or treaters', but also for the 1,000 accompanying parents and grandparents, who avidly participate in all the game booths provided.

Spooktacular isn't just a celebration of Hallowe'en, it's a celebration of the spirit of Penticton.

Penticton Community Centre

Rod Penfold

The Kettle Valley Railway ran from Midway to Hope. East of the Okanagan it climbed to a 4,000 ft. summit, winding through three–fingered Myra Canyon. The steep walls necessitated 17 trestles and two tunnels, measuring one and a half miles, to accommodate the six mile passage across the Canyon. This section of the KVR has been designated as part of the Trans Canada Trail. Both these modes of transportation took our men off to World War 1. Our naturally grown wild poppies (facing page) are a sign of remembrance.

The S.S. Sicamous was launched from Okanagan Landing (5 miles west of Vernon) on May 19, 1914. The maiden voyage on June 12, 1914 carried numerous dignitaries on a six hour trip from Okanagan Landing to Penticton. The paddle–wheeler could carry nearly 500 passengers. Its last run was in July, 1937. The Sicamous went into dry dock in Penticton on August 27, 1951, where it sits today as a 'living museum'. It houses one of the largest 'HO' Gauge miniature railways (the KVR) in Western Canada.

Joey Walker

Penticton Museum Archives

Shelley R. Daly

Dan Lybarger

Nestled in the heart of the city lies a beautiful stone heritage home known as Leir House (facing page). This was the first home of the Leir family and was later converted to a nurses' residence until 1979 when it became a centre for arts and culture. Within its walls are housed numerous groups, such as the Penticton Music Academy, the Multicultural Society, the Potters Guild, and the Arts Council.

Rod Penfold

Penticton Secondary School is comprised of three buildings – the Main (the biggest of them all), the Ellis and the Shatford. The Ellis building (photo) was built in 1913, originally as an elementary school. In 1921, the Shatford was built as a Junior High. The original high school was located across the street on the site of the present–day Library/Museum Complex location.

Today, the school is a hub of teenage academics, theatre, and sports activities. There are numerous quality education facilities from which the residents can choose. These include French immersion, private, public and post secondary institutions such as Okanagan University College. The "Dry Grad" celebrations for high school graduating classes, which first began in Penticton, has been readily adopted by other communities.

Harry Killick

It's not always summer in the Okanagan, and winter has its own charm as seen in this 1950s photo (facing page) of Lakeshore Drive.

courtesy Frances Lougheed Harry Davis – Cameo Photo Supplies

Only fours years after Memorial Arena opened its doors, our city became world renown for hockey. The Penticton Vees, a Senior AA hockey team, beat the Sudbury Wolves in the 1953/54 season, winning the Canadian Allan Cup.

For winning this cup the Vees were chosen to represent Canada at the 1955 World Hockey Championship held in Germany. Their devoted fans were not disappointed! While many of the players' wives listened to games on the radio at home, the Vees played a total of eight teams in the A division, winning every game. They went on to meet the defending champions, the Russians, and beat them 5 – 0 in the final game. The town went wild when the Vees returned to Penticton as the new World Champions.

David Szabo

Jack Frost touches our shores briefly. When he does, locals respond by enjoying various activities in the newly remodelled Memorial Arena (facing page), or donning skates and sticks for outdoor play on the frozen lakes.

Hockey remains a favourite pastime for all ages. Many a Saturday is taken up with families cheering on their young daughters and sons in minor hockey or cheering on the junior hockey team that same evening. Some of these families are also involved in the more graceful, yet equally skilful, sport of figure–skating.

Many NHL and international hockey players have launched their career after playing on Penticton's junior team or attending the Okanagan Hockey School, which has made its home here for over 35 years.

Sport history buffs enjoy a step back in time while visiting The Hockey Wall of Fame housed in Memorial Arena.

Frank Babakaiff

For the daring, the annual Polar Bear Dip gets a person's blood circulating!

Gerhard Kahrmann

Chris Cornett

Snow lovers find a winter wonderland only 20 short minutes from town at the local ski resort. Lovers sneak away for a romantic weekend or families spend their Christmas vacation in a cozy mountain chalet. Enthusiasts participate in a high quality downhill or cross-country ski experience in "champagne" powder unique to the mountains of the Okanagan Valley. All ages can participate in the fun which includes snowmobiling and snowboarding.

Penticton offers the best of both worlds for skiers and golfers. In early spring, one can take in a morning of skiing, and pick up a round of golf in the afternoon at one of the local courses.

For a serene finish to the day, a sleigh ride fits the bill.

Chris Cornett

Gerhard Kahrmann

Bighorn sheep, indigenous to this area, are seen more frequently at lower levels as they come down the slopes in search of food and water. This mild–mannered form of wildlife is seen year–round.

Most wildlife enjoy a siesta during the cooler months, but those who are lucky might catch a glimpse of a 'snow bunny' during a cross-country ski run.

Gerhard Kahrmann

Rod Penfold

OGOPOGO IS THE SEA CREATURE OF PENTICTON.

GETS TO SEE ALL OF THE TOURISTS!

OGOPOGO HAS NEVER BEEN SEEN.

PEOPLE ARE ALWAYS LOOKING FOR IT.

OGOPOGO IS VERY SNEAKY AND MYSTERIOUS.

GOES AROUND THE WHOLE OKANAGAN LAKE.

OGOPOGO IS THE SAME SPELT BOTH WAYS-
O-G-O-P-O-G-O!!

Emily Gray Age 12, Grade 7

LAKE OKANAGAN

by Clement Battye, Penticton pioneer

In the land of sky blue waters,
Nature's paradise supreme,
Nestles Okanagan Valley,
Vale of Lakes and forests green.

Streams of sparkling, spring–fed water,
Amble down to sunny bays,
Morning sunbeams light the shadows,
Through the early morning haze.

Nestled in that gorgeous valley,
Gem of myriad sky–blue lakes,
Okanagan's breathless beauty,
Before the wanderer's vision breaks.

Mirrored surface of the water,
Reflects the beauty of the scene,
Of mountain crags, majestic grandeur,
Forest glades, a sea of green.

Bounteous nature has been lavish,
Has indeed endowed this land,
Surely so much beauty must be,
Fashioned by a master hand.

To every thing there is a season . . .

courtesy Penticton Museum Les Hill collection

PHOTOGRAPH CONTRIBUTORS

Aerro Photography (Shelley R. Daly)

Cameo Photo Supplies-Harry Davis - Frances Lougheed

Dan Lybarger Photography

David Szabo Photography

Doug Cox

Frank Babakaiff

Gerhard Kahrmann

Harry Killick

Hillmen M. Holm

Howie Richardson

Jeanette Beaven, Dragon's Den

Joey Walker, Wildling Photophilosophy

John & Donna Ortiz (Riordan House B & B)

Laure Neish

Nikos Theodosakis

Penticton Community Centre

Penticton Herald - John Moorhouse

Penticton Museum Archives

Penticton Museum, Les Hill Collection

Photography by Chris Cornett

Randy Manuel

Richard J. Cannings

Rod Penfold

Steven Tomlinson Photography

Stewart Lyon

Stuart Bish M.P.A. Photography/Design

Sumac Ridge Estate Winery Ltd.

The Film Box

Tourism Penticton

SPONSORS

Art Knapp's Plantland and Flower Shop
BDO Dunwoody
Belisle, Penticton
Berry & Smith Trucking
Best Western Inn at Penticton
Bob Brown Pontiac Buick Ltd.
Boult & Sons Automotive Ltd.
Boyle & Co.-James W. Dewdney
British Columbia Wine Information Centre
Canada Trust
Canadian Imperial Bank of Commerce-Penticton
Canadian Mental Health Association
Canadian Tire and Service Centre
Canwood Furniture Inc.
Cantex Engineering & Construction Co. Ltd.
CFUW Penticton-University Women's Club
Charles Albas Law Corp.
Christopher and Jocelyn Wood & Family
C.I.B.C. Wood Gundy Securities Incorporated
City Department Head Group
City of Penticton
Coldwell Banker OKanagan Realty
Coyote Cruises
Cumming Jamieson Ltd.-Insurance Brokers
David & Michou Szabo
Dawn & Gary Denton
Doc's Computers
Dr. Robert & Mrs. Marg Abbey
Dr. David and Sig Novak
Dr. I.R. Dickinson
Dr. R.R. Blanchard & Staff
Family of John Duncan (1998 Man of the Year)
Fine Line (1998) General Contractors
G. Little Group
God's Mountain Crest Chalet/Showcase Bistro
Greenwood Forest Products
Greyback Construction Ltd./ Kenyon & Co. Ltd.
Guerard Fine Furniture
Gyro Club of Penticton
Halbauer & Co.
International Order of Job's Daughters Bethel #16
Investors Group
Jackson Triggs Wines-Vincor International Corp.
Jason Eastwood/North Shore Fitness
Jim Hart M.P. Okanagan-Coquihalla
John & Donna Ortiz-Riordan House Bed & Breakfast
Keith Bevington/Margaret Leck-Remax Penticton Realty
Kemp Harvey Lister Inc.
Knights of Columbus Council #3127
KPMG
Lloyd Gallery
Moduline Industries
New System Printing & Copying
Okanagan Boat Charters
Parker's Chrysler Dodge Jeep
Pen High After Grad
Penticton & District Multicultural Society
Penticton & Wine Country Chamber of Commerce
Penticton Business & Professional Women
Penticton Herald/SOUTHERN exposure
Penticton Honda/Penticton Motor Products Ltd.
Penticton IGA
Penticton Inn & Conference Centre
Penticton Lakeside Resort
Penticton Masonic Lodge No. 147
Penticton Minor Hockey Concession
Penticton Morning News
Penticton Plaza Shopping Centre
Penticton Public Library
Penticton Self Storage
Penticton Seniors' Recreation and Wellness Centre
Penticton Toyota Leisureland Inc.
Penticton Trade & Convention Centre
Penticton Western News Advertiser
Penticton Writers and Publishers
Peters Bros Construction Ltd.
Pythian Sisters Calanthe Temple #26
Ramada Courtyard Inn
Rick Thorpe M.L.A. Okanagan-Penticton
Rita & Jim O'Neill
Royal Bank Financial Group
Royal Canadian Mounted Police
S.S. Sicamous Society
Sentes Chevrolet-Oldsmobile-Cadillac Ltd.
Sherwood Trophies & Signs Ltd.
Snow Mountain Market
South Okanagan Similkameen Brain Injury Society
South Okanagan Roofing
Subaru Ironman Canada Triathlon Championship
Sumac Ridge Estate Winery Ltd.
Sunlakes Consulting Group
Sutton Group Skaha Realty-Real Estate Specialists
TD Bank Financial Group
The Thorpe Family
Theo's Restaurant Ltd.
Tourism Penticton
Weyerhaeuser Canada Ltd.
Wolfram Developments Ltd.
Yost Winter Insurance Agencies Ltd.

Retail Sponsors

Books N'Things (1974) Ltd.
Bugsy's Artisan Crafts & Giftware
Coles Book Store Limited
Okanagan Books
Overwaitea Book Store
Smartshopper Discount-Penticton's Largest Dollar Store
Terwilliger P. Jones Gifts